Inside My Body

Why do my ears pop?

Ann Fullick

www.raintreepublishers.co.uk
Visit our website to find out more information about Raintree books.

To order:
☎ Phone 0845 6044371
📄 Fax +44 (0) 1865 312263
💻 Email myorders@raintreepublishers.co.uk

Customers from outside the UK please telephone +44 1865 312262

Raintree is an imprint of Capstone Global Library Limited, a company incorporated in England and Wales having its registered office at 7 Pilgrim Street, London, EC4V 6LB – Registered company number: 6695582

Edited by Kate de Villiers and Vaarunika Dharmapala
Designed by Steve Mead
Illustrations by KJA-Artists.com
Picture research by Mica Brancic
Originated by Capstone Global Library Ltd
Printed and bound in China by CTPS

ISBN 978 1 406 22105 3 (hardback)
15 14 13 12 11
10 9 8 7 6 5 4 3 2 1

British Library Cataloguing in Publication Data
Fullick, Ann
Why do my ears pop?. -- (Inside my body)
612.8'5-dc22
A full catalogue record for this book is available from the British Library.

Acknowledgements
We would like to thank the following for permission to reproduce photographs: Alamy pp. **15** (© MedicalRF.com), **19** (© Custom Medical Stock Photo); Corbis pp. **6** (PhotoAlto/© Laurence Mouton), **22** (© LWA-Sharie Kennedy); Getty Images pp. **7** (AFP/Berthold Stadler), **17** (Bloomberg), **26** (Taxi/Chris Clinton); Getty Images news p. **27** (Sandy Huffaker); iStockphoto.com pp. **4** (© Björn Kindler), **18** (© Roger Jegg), **20** (© Edward Bock), **24** (© sambrogio); Science Photo Library pp. **13** (Dr Richard Kessel & Dr Gene Shih, Visuals Unlimited), **16** (CC, ISM), **21** (Medical RF.Com), **25** (CC, ISM); Shutterstock pp. **4 band aid** (© Isaac Marzioli), **4 gauze** (© Yurok), **8** (Joshua David Treisner), **9** (© jaana piira), **25 band aid** (© Isaac Marzioli), **25 gauze** (© Yurok).

Cover photograph of a boy with his fingers in his ears reproduced with permission of Corbis (© Rob Lewine).

We would like to thank David Wright for his invaluable help in the preparation of this book.

Every effort has been made to contact copyright holders of any material reproduced in this book. Any omissions will be rectified in subsequent printings if notice is given to the publisher.

Disclaimer
All the internet addresses (URLs) given in this book were valid at the time of going to press. However, due to the dynamic nature of the internet, some addresses may have changed, or sites may have changed or ceased to exist since publication. While the author and publisher regret any inconvenience this may cause readers, no responsibility for any such changes can be accepted by either the author or the publisher.

Contents

Words that appear in the text in bold, **like this**, are explained in the glossary on page 30.

Why do my ears pop?

When you take off in an aeroplane, walk up a mountain, or dive underwater, your ears can hurt. You cannot hear very well. Then your ears pop, and all is well. Why do your ears pop?

Practical advice

Suck a sweet!

You are often given sweets to suck in a plane as it takes off and lands. Sucking and swallowing helps your ears to pop and stops them hurting. Chewing gum and yawning can help, too.

Air pressure

The **air pressure** inside your ear needs to be the same as the air pressure outside your body. As you land in a plane, the air pressure outside changes and this can hurt your ear. When you swallow, your **Eustachian tube** opens up and air moves into your ear with a pop. Now you feel better!

You can change the air pressure in your ears. Breath in, hold your nose tightly, close your mouth, and try to push the air gently but firmly down your nose. You should hear your ears go pop!

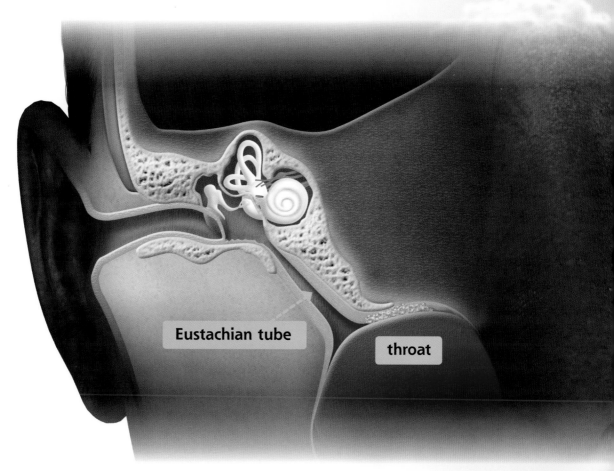

Eustachian tube

throat

This is where your Eustachian tube is.

What do **ears do?**

Your ears are amazing. You have an outer ear, a middle ear, and an inner ear. In this book you are going to find out what your ears do and how all the different parts work.

🔍 **Your ears help you hear what your friends say.**

Hearing

You hear sound using your ears. Be very quiet and listen. You can hear very quiet sounds, like a cat purring or a clock ticking. You can also hear very loud sounds such as music or thunder. You talk to your parents, your teachers, and your friends. You can hear danger, such as when a car is coming along the street. How many times have your ears kept you safe?

Moving

Your ears do more than allow you to hear. Special parts in your inner ear sense when you are moving around. Later, you will find out how this can make you feel dizzy!

Balance

Without your ears you cannot balance properly. Your inner ear has senses that tell your brain which way up you are, and whether you are moving your head about. If these do not work properly you feel very dizzy. You might even fall over or be sick!

Dancers use their ears to hear music, to move, and to balance.

What is Sound?

Bang a drum and the skin on the top of the drum **vibrates**. It moves up and down. It pushes the air around it back and forth and makes the air vibrate, too. This is sound. Sound vibrations can travel through air.

When you pluck a guitar string, you can see the vibrations which make the sound.

Hearing sounds

Sound can also travel through liquids and solids. You can hear sound travel though solids. Put your ear on the table, stretch out your hand, and knock gently on the table top.

Your ears can hear sounds in the air best. They do not work so well underwater. Some sounds are so loud they can hurt your ears, for instance loud music, or a police siren.

Extreme body fact

Loudest animal sounds

Sounds are measured in decibels. One of the loudest animal sounds is made by the blue whale. It is 188 decibels and can travel hundreds of kilometres underwater. The loudest shout a human can make is about 80 decibels!

Howler monkeys make loud sounds of about 88 decibels. Their sounds carry through the forest to tell other monkeys where they live.

What is my outer ear?

The outer ear is made up of the **pinna**, the ear canal, and the **eardrum**. The pinnae are the flaps of skin that stick out from either side of your head. Leading from each of these is an ear canal. This is a tube that goes inside your head. At the end of each ear canal is an eardrum, which closes off the outer ear from the middle ear.

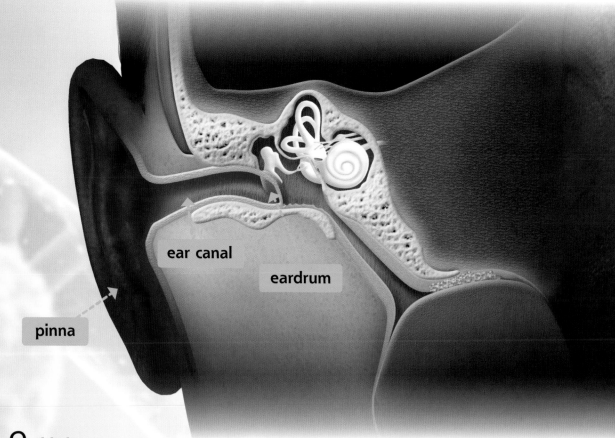

ear canal

eardrum

pinna

🔍 This is your outer ear.

Your eardrum is like a drum skin. When sounds go into your ear they make your eardrum **vibrate**.

The pinna helps to catch sounds. It also helps you to tell which direction a sound is coming from. Close your eyes and listen. If someone talks, you can tell where they are by the sound of their voice!

Ear wax

Your ear makes ear wax to protect the skin inside the ear canal. The wax moves out of your ear, taking any dirt with it. If your ear makes too much wax it can block your ear and stop you hearing clearly.

 SCIENCE BEHIND THE **MYTH**

MYTH: Olive oil cures earache.

SCIENCE: It's true! Doctors have proved that warm oils soften hard earwax so it comes out and your ear stops hurting. Your doctor will tell you if this is right for you. It is a bit messy so do not try it at home unless your parents say that you can!

Why are there bones in my ear?

Inside your ear, in your middle ear, you have three small bones known as **ossicles**. They are also called the hammer, the anvil, and the stirrup. When a sound makes your **eardrum vibrate**, this in turn makes the hammer move. The hammer bangs into the anvil, and the anvil moves the stirrup. As the three little bones rock together, they pass the vibration across your middle ear to your inner ear.

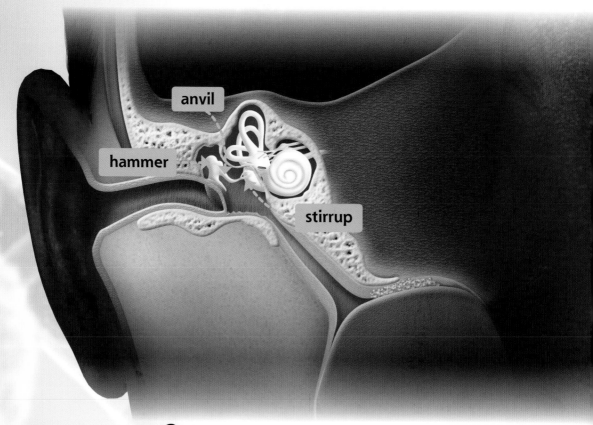

anvil

hammer

stirrup

🔎 **This is your middle ear.**

Your middle ear is usually filled with air. If you get an ear infection, your middle ear may fill up with liquid. When this happens, the little bones cannot rock so well. This means you will not be able to hear as well as usual.

Replacing the bones

Sometimes a person's ear bones can join together or crumble away so they cannot hear. Scientists and doctors have made tiny replacement bones from special chemicals. Surgeons operate on your middle ear and put the new "bones" in place. Then you can hear again!

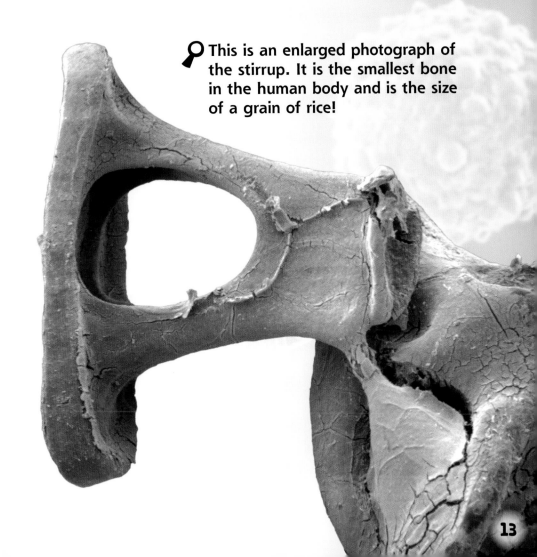

This is an enlarged photograph of the stirrup. It is the smallest bone in the human body and is the size of a grain of rice!

How do I hear?

Now we are going to look deep inside your ear, right into the inner ear.

You hear because sound **vibrations** are picked up by **auditory nerves** in your **cochlea**. Vibrations move through the air, from your **eardrum** across the tiny bones of your middle ear to your inner ear. Here they move into the cochlea, which is full of liquid.

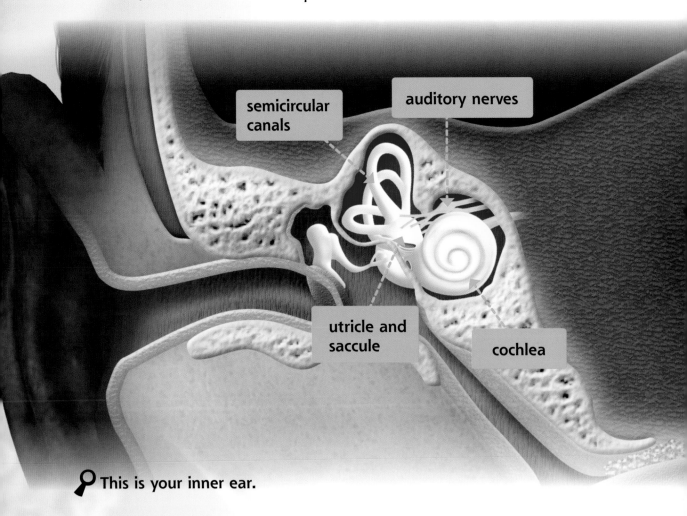

semicircular canals

auditory nerves

utricle and saccule

cochlea

This is your inner ear.

Hairy ears

The sound vibrations move through the liquid like waves. Inside the cochlea there are hairs which join on to nerve endings. As the vibrations move through the liquid, they move the hairs. Nerve messages are sent from the cochlea to the brain. They travel along the auditory nerves.

The messages from the auditory nerves are taken to a special part of your brain. This is how you hear sounds.

Extreme body fact

Hidden length!
Your cochlea is the size of a pea when it is coiled up. If you stretch it out, it is almost 4 centimetres (1.6 inches) long!

The cochlea looks like a snail shell.

What makes hearing difficult?

Anything which stops sound **vibrations** travelling from your outer ear to your inner ear makes hearing difficult. Wax in your outer ear can do this, as can an ear infection which fills your middle ear with fluid.

Sometimes your **eardrum** gets a hole in it. This is called a burst eardrum. It might be because you have hit your head, or because you have a middle ear infection. Without your eardrum, you cannot hear in that ear. All of these problems get better on their own or with treatment from the doctor.

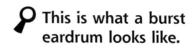

This is what a burst eardrum looks like.

Deafness

If you cannot hear, you are said to be deaf. Some deaf people can hear nothing at all, but others can hear some sounds. Sometimes babies are born deaf. Their **auditory nerves** may not work, or parts of their middle or inner ear may be missing.

Some people can hear when they are born, but lose their hearing later. Bad infections can make you deaf for the rest of your life. As people get older their auditory nerves often do not work as well as they used to. This makes hearing difficult.

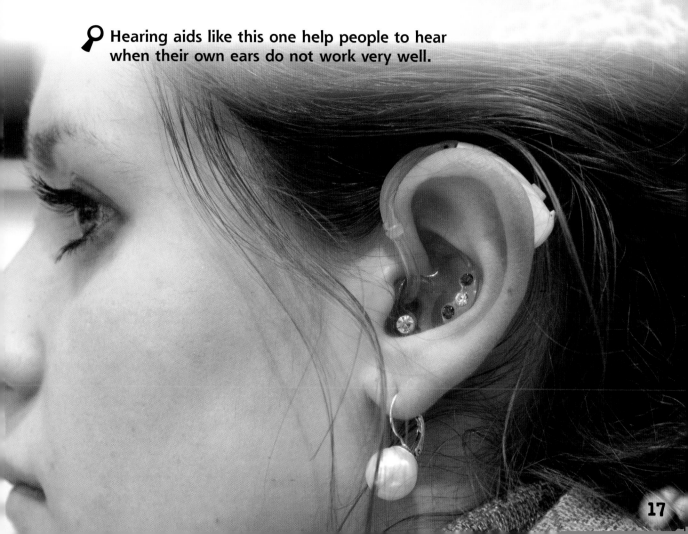

🔎 Hearing aids like this one help people to hear when their own ears do not work very well.

Does music hurt my ears?

Most people enjoy listening to music. But can it hurt your hearing?

At concerts and parties, the sound coming out of the speakers can be so loud that it can damage the little hairs in your **cochlea**. You cannot hear very well for a while afterwards. If you are close to the speakers for too long your ears may not get better.

You can enjoy listening to music without damaging your ears. Keep the sound at a safe level.

MP3 players

MP3 players are great. You can choose your own music and turn it up over the sound of traffic or people talking. But be careful that the music is not so loud that it could damage your ears. Doctors worry that many young people will damage their hearing because they play their MP3 players too loud.

🔍 Tinnitus, a constant noise in your ear, is one hearing problem that can be caused by listening to too much loud music.

Extreme body fact

MP3s can hurt!
Sounds of 80 decibels can hurt your ears. Some MP3 players reach 105 decibels, which is as loud as the sound a chainsaw makes!

How do I balance?

You can stand on one leg, put your head on one side, and look from side to side, all without falling over! How do you keep your balance? Many parts of your body help out, but the **sense organs** in your inner ear are also very important. These organs are the **utricle** and **saccule**, and the **semicircular canals**.

🔍 You can see how well the sense organs work by looking at this gymnast. She is balanced on a beam.

Balancing

The utricle and saccule help you know which way up your head and body are. They also detect when the head is moving forwards, backwards, or is nodding. The utricle and saccule are filled with fluid and contain jelly-like blobs attached to hairs. When you move about the fluid and jelly blobs also move and tug on the hairs. This sends a message to your brain, which helps you to keep your balance during movement.

Infection

If you get an infection in the sense organs of your inner ear, you can feel very dizzy even when you are sitting still. If you stand up you may feel so dizzy that you fall over! Luckily, this can be easily cured by visiting a doctor.

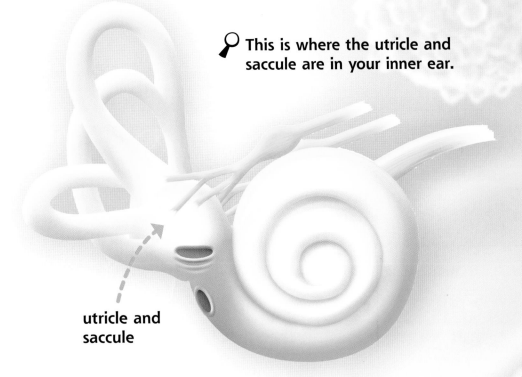

🔍 This is where the utricle and saccule are in your inner ear.

utricle and saccule

Why do I get dizzy?

Spin around and around, and then stop. It will feel as if you are still spinning around!

🔍 **Spinning makes you feel dizzy!**

Movement

Your inner ear contains three **semicircular canals**. One goes up, one goes down, and one goes across. As in the **utricle** and **saccule**, each canal is filled with fluid and contains jelly-like blobs attached to hairs. As you move around, the fluid and jelly-like blobs tug on the hairs. This sends a message to your brain. Your brain then knows that you are moving, and the direction you are moving in.

Dizziness

When you spin around, the fluid in your semicircular canals spins, too. When you stop spinning, the liquid keeps going. Your eyes tell your brain you are not moving, but your semicircular canals tell your brain you are spinning. This is why you feel dizzy! As soon as the liquid in your semicircular canals stops moving, you stop feeling dizzy.

Extreme body fact

Dizzy dancers
Dancers spin around a lot but do not get dizzy. How? The dancer stares at one spot then turns her head in a quick move. Her head stays in one place most of the time. This stops her getting dizzy.

🔍 **This is where the semicircular canals are in your inner ear.**

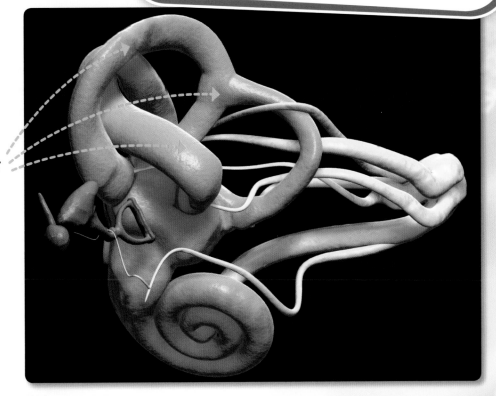

semicircular canals

How can I look after my ears?

If you look after your ears, you can help to protect your hearing. Here are some useful tips:

- Keep your ears clean and dry.
- Never poke things into your ears. You might hurt your **eardrum**.
- Listen to music sensibly. Remember that very loud music can make it harder for you to hear well.
- Water in dirty swimming pools can carry germs and cause infection. When you go swimming, protect your ears with earplugs.

This boy is making sure his earplugs are in place while he plays in a swimming pool.

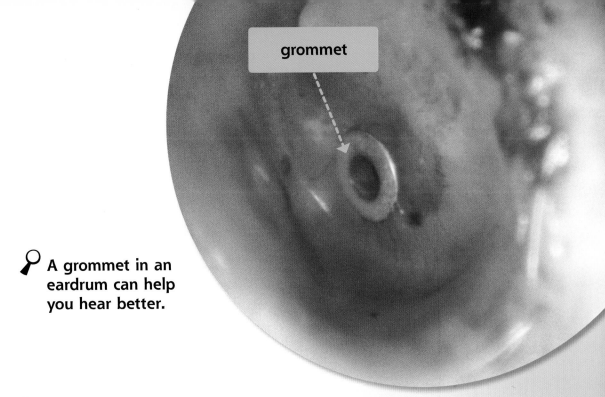

grommet

 A grommet in an eardrum can help you hear better.

Glue ear

Some children have a problem called glue ear. This is when too much fluid gets into the middle ear and cannot flow down the **Eustachian tube**. The problem is fixed using grommets. These are small, plastic valves that allow the fluid to drain out through the eardrum until the Eustachian tube grows big enough to work on its own.

SCIENCE BEHIND THE MYTH

MYTH: Earwigs can climb into your ears and eat your brains.

SCIENCE: No, they can't! Earwigs do not climb into human ears. However, doctors do find many strange things in children's ears, such as food, beads, small toys, and insects. The child has usually put the object in his or her own ear!

Ears are amazing!

On each side of your head you have an ear. They are full of surprises! You have an outer ear, a middle ear, and an inner ear.

Sound, balance, and movement

Your outer ear catches sound and takes it into the rest of your ear. Your middle ear contains small bones which carry the sound waves into your inner ear.

🔍 Your ears let you hear everything from a whisper to a warning shout. Hearing is a very precious sense.

Your inner ear holds the **cochlea**, the part that is sensitive to sounds. It also contains the **utricle**, **saccule**, and the **semicircular canals**. These help you to balance, and to know where your body is and when you are moving!

Every time you talk to your friends, or stand on your head, or enjoy the dizzy feeling after a ride at a theme park, remember to thank your ears. They are truly amazing!

Your ears tell you which way up you are, even on a roller coaster!

All about ears

A dog's squeaky toy can make a sound of 135 decibels. That is loud enough to damage your hearing if the squeaking goes on too long.

Your ears continue to grow throughout your life. They grow almost two millimetres every nine years!

Modern hearing aids are very small and can be hidden inside or behind your ear (see page 17). In the 1800s and early 1900s, people used ear trumpets to help them hear. These were big, often 30 centimetres (1 foot) long!

Some people have hissing, roaring, clicking, or ringing noises in their ears all the time. They are not hearing things. They have a condition called tinnitus (see page 19).

An Indian man named Anthony Victor has the longest recorded hair growing out of his ears. It is 18.1 centimetres (7.12 inches) long!

Parts of the ear

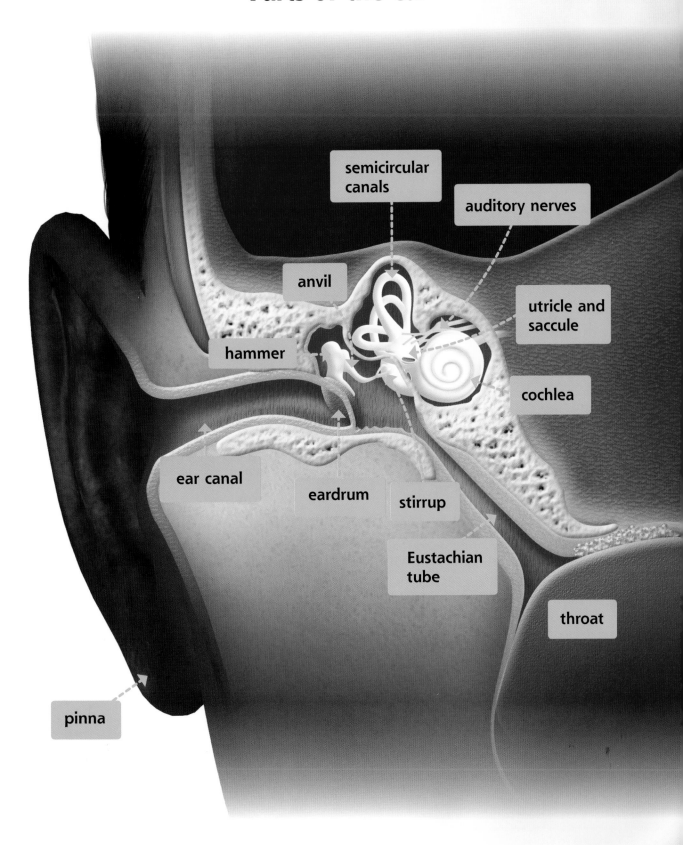

semicircular
canals

auditory nerves

anvil

utricle and
saccule

hammer

cochlea

ear canal

eardrum

stirrup

Eustachian
tube

throat

pinna

Glossary

air pressure push of air against objects

auditory nerve part that carries messages from the cochlea to the brain

cochlea coiled part of the inner ear which picks up sound

eardrum found between the outer and middle ear. The eardrum passes sound to the bones of the middle ear.

Eustachian tube tube which joins the middle ear to the back of the throat

ossicle one of three small bones in the middle ear, also called the hammer, the anvil, and the stirrup

pinna (more than one: **pinnae**) flap of skin found on either side of the head

saccule part of the inner ear that helps with balance and movement

semicircular canal part of the inner ear that helps with balance and movement

sense organ part of the body that makes you aware of your surroundings. Your ears and eyes are sense organs.

utricle part of the inner ear that helps with balance and movement

vibrate when something shakes very fast, usually many times a second

Find out more

Books

Encyclopedia of the Human Body (Dorling Kindersley, 2010)

Jordan Has a Hearing Loss (Like Me, Like You), Jillian Powell (Evans Brothers, 2009)

The Human Body Book: An Illustrated Guide, Steve Parker (Dorling Kindersley, 2007)

Websites

www.bbc.co.uk/science/humanbody/body/factfiles/hearing/hearing_animation.shtml

Visit this website to see an animation of how we hear.

www.ndcs.org.uk/help_us/schools_fundraising/fingerspellathon/index.html

Get your school involved in a "fingerspellathon" and learn more about how deaf people use sign language.

www.childrenfirst.nhs.uk/kids/health/body_tour/ears.html

Take a tour around the human body on this website. See what more you can discover about your ears.

Index

PILLGWENLLY.

23-07-18.